Minimalism & Color
DesignSource

MINIMALISM & COLOR DESIGNSOURCE
Copyright © 2009 COLLINS DESIGN and LOFT Publications

HarperCollins books may be purchased for educational, business, or sales promotional use.
For information, please write: Special Markets Department, HarperCollins*Publishers*,
10 East 53rd Street, New York, NY 10022.

First Edition published in 2009 by
Collins Design
An Imprint of HarperCollins*Publishers*
10 East 53rd Street
New York, NY 10022
Tel.: (212) 207-7000
Fax: (212) 207-7654
collinsdesign@harpercollins.com
www.harpercollins.com

Distributed throughout the world by
HarperCollins*Publishers*
10 East 53rd Street
New York, NY 10022
Fax: (212) 207-7654

Packaged by
LOFT Publications
Via Laietana 32, 4° Of. 92
08003 Barcelona, Spain
Tel.: +34 932 688 088
Fax: +34 932 687 073
loft@loftpublications.com
www.loftpublications.com

Editorial coordination:
Catherine Collin

Editor:
Aitana Lleonart

Art director:
Mireia Casanovas Soley

Cover design:
Claudia Martínez Alonso

Layout:
Esperanza Escudero

Library of Congress Control Number: 2008937643
ISBN: 978-0-06-154280-0

Printed in Spain

Minimalism & Color
DesignSource

COLLINS DESIGN
An Imprint of HarperCollinsPublishers

Introduction

The term "minimalism" was born supposedly to define art that aimed to not be identified either with painting or sculpture and which eventually ended up becoming a global concept. However, its application has prevailed particularly in the fields of architecture and interior design. Use of the word is attributed to British critic Richard Wollheim, who coined it in a 1965 article that attempted to define the reductionist trend in art. During this period, when the trend began to form its own identity, other expressions and formulas arose to refer to it but they fell into disuse or did not manage to catch on. To refer to this search for the essential which is aimed at the reduction of forms to their most elementary—an idea that had already begun with rationalism—various expressions were fielded, such as "ABC art," "rejective art" and "reductivism." The term "minimalism" therefore made a space for itself and went on to become incontrovertibly linked with a well-known phrase attributed to the architect and designer Mies van der Rohe, who also led the Bauhaus School. This phrase is, of course, "Less is more"—a definition that will go down in posterity as the best and most austere formula for defining a similarly austere aesthetic current.

Although minimalism appeared in the 1960s, it did not really take off until the 1970s. It was a clear reaction against previous art forms, including the unrestrained use of color and the features of pop art, as well as other trends of the time. This phenomenon has been repeated throughout history. Artistic movements could be compared with the movement of a pendulum, which oscillates from one extreme to the other: from Gothic to Renaissance, Neo-Classicism to Romanticism and pop art to minimalism, with its eagerness to return to the essential; putting purity and the simplicity of lines above all else. Minimalism could therefore be defined as the art of stripping a thing of its surplus or unnecessary elements.

Within the minimalist current, the application and treatment of color becomes a fundamental and even determining element. In its most dogmatic version, minimalism should go hand-in-hand with absolute monochromie. Each space would involve a single color on the floors, ceilings and walls, and the contrast would be provided only from the furniture and accessories, which should never be overdone. The nuance of minimalism lies more in structures and forms than accessories. The austerity, purism, simplicity and dematerialization that define it should be matched with a particular use of color that emphasizes its character or plays only with subtly unbalancing its harmony. In any décor based on a minimalist style, the contrast between black and white is the best bet. The luminous nature of white, which is in essence the sum of all colors, stands in sharp contrast with the absence of color, i.e., what we call "black." The two are opposites, but their union results in a noticeable sobriety and aesthetic purity.

As well as this major pairing, which should be given prime importance, each color and type of combination can endow a minimalist space with a distinct personality. They can convey serenity, excitement, harmony, strength and even balance. To better understand the effect of each color—which is awarded psychological factors that color psychology studies exhaustively—it is necessary to use a color wheel, which features the primary colors (red, yellow and blue) along with the secondary and intermediary colors and shows the complementary colors which, despite being situated at the opposite end of the chart, offer the most harmonious combinations.

All of this theory is indispensable when it comes to choosing the color range to decorate any space, as this selection and the combination of colors will determine the final result and the sensory perception of the space. When you use white in combination with another tone, it will be the latter that conveys the personality via the decoration. If it is red, for example, it will exude brightness, strength and vigor; if green or yellow, tranquility and concentration; while pale blues reflect serenity and relaxation. The combination of two colors other than black and white is more complicated: if it involves complementary colors the result may be a harmonious space, but otherwise it is possible it will be overwhelming and too elaborate. A large part of the weight also depends on the shades, as they will determine the perception of the environment. In short, color and its combinations can still be used to create spaces inspired by minimalism, which seek to maintain its essence and purest form.

Color Wheel

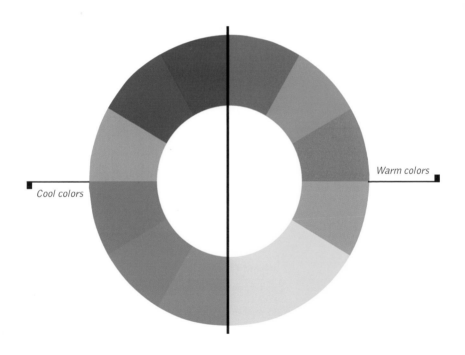

Warm colors

Cool colors

Complementary Colors

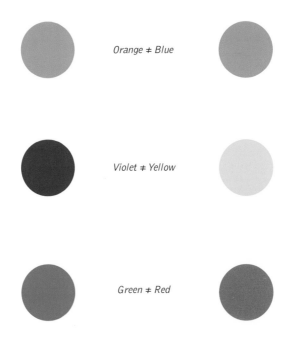

Orange ≠ Blue

Violet ≠ Yellow

Green ≠ Red

Black & White:
Absence of Color and Color Addition

The chromatic essence of minimalism

In décor based on a minimalist style and its theories, the combination and contrast between black and white is its most pure expression. The elegance and simplicity of the two colors reinforce the minimalist purity of structures, furniture and decorative elements. Black and white creates a play of antagonism, of contrasts, in any space, where elegance becomes the key ally.

Calm, tranquility and harmony are often associated with the color white. Its use in decoration has always been linked to these feelings, as its psychological effect is at all times positive; that is why it is commonly used in spaces earmarked for relaxing therapy or beauty treatments. It involves the sum or synthesis of all the colors and is the one that is most light-sensitive.

Black presents a symbolic duality. On the one hand it is related with the mysterious and even the impure or malign. However, it is also synonymous with elegance, nobility and sobriety, as well as power and authority. In decoration it is more common to find it in ornaments and details than on large surfaces or walls as, because it does not reflect the light, it can reduce the feeling of space in a room. Sometimes, when a room is designed with a color range based on this combination, black tones are used in the flooring, so that the white walls can reign visually. Black, in combination with bright clear colors such as orange, yellow or, in this case, white, has a vigorous and energetic effect.

From the fusion of the absence of color, i.e., black, and the synthesis of them all, i.e., white, we obtain the color gray. Its tone and intensity depends on the proportions of the mix. It can be a perfect union between the elegance of black and the luminosity of white, adapting to any decorative style as it is a neutral tone. All its colors and tones reinforce the purity and sobriety of minimalist lines perfectly. The secret, in short, is to combine it well, highlighting its main features and at the same time transmitting (despite its apparent neutrality) strength and personality.

If a design in fine and simple lines is
added to the neutral character of these
two colors, the effect is of an absolutely
minimalist and essential decor.

The clear predominance of black makes the overall look too somber, so it is necessary to achieve a balance between the two tones.

The strength and character of these two
colors is palpable simply by applying a
dash of one to the other, as the contrast
lends personality to any piece
or ambiance.

This chromatic duality applied in spaces
like the kitchen or bathroom is very
elegant and balanced.

A scarcity of furniture and the
spaciousness of the room to decorate
make it possible to opt for furniture of
a bolder design and fabric, as austerity
and simplicity will still reign.

Some of the most important pieces in
any décor are chairs, armchairs and
couches, basic elements whose design
makes a significant contribution to the
interior-design purpose.

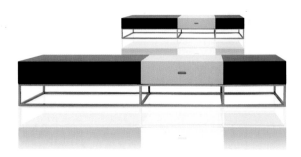

Sideboards are a great idea for storing
tableware. If in neutral tones, they can
also integrate with the rest of the décor.

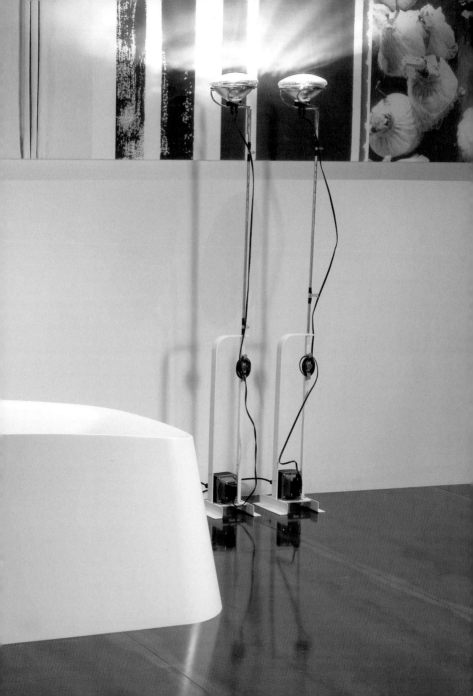

■

Combining black and white is a perfect
way to break up the uniformity and
monotony of a space without drastically
altering its visual harmony.

Black and white is the minimalist mix
par excellence. If you also add small
pieces of furniture the space will be
a magnificent example of this style.

The material that best complements this
chromatic duo is undoubtedly metal,
perceived as an intermediate gray tone
that also reflects the light.

■

Sometimes accessories can add a note
of contrast to particular designs, such
as couch cushions or a side table.

Between black and white is a whole
scale of grays, a color whose tones
—because they are also neutral—
can be applied without affecting
the color harmony.

Straight, clean-lined furniture can
convey a feeling of balance and
harmony not just through its tones but
also its shape.

■

To divide different areas of use in the
same space, one of the most practical
solutions is screens, which should be
noticeable but not draw too much
attention to themselves.

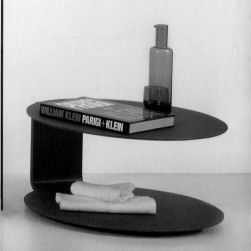

While black adds a sober touch,
white makes the most of the natural
light, absorbing and reverberating
with the sunlight.

A very simple but effective decorative
recourse is to alternate the parts of
the couch or relaxation areas in
black and white.

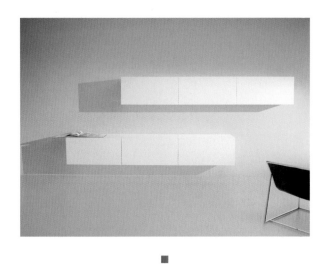

In the living room, items like the couch
and TV module are of key significance.
Choose a neutral tone so they can adapt
to any possible changes in decoration.

The kitchen is a space where
functionality is of prime importance,
so its distribution should be comfortable
and agile. The combination of these two
tones also makes it look nice and clean.

To play with more shades in these two
tones, try different materials and
finishes such as matte or lacquer.

In spaces reserved for relaxation, such as the living room or bedroom, it is better for the contrast between the two colors to be subtler, to prevent an overly aggressive result.

Despite the search for simplicity and
purity, you can still use patterns with the
minimalist look, as some have very
subtle shapes and combinations.

Suspended furniture frees up space
to move in. If in neutral colors, it will
blend into the walls and not stand
out too much.

■

When you apply a dark color like black
to a wall it is best to do so on just one
surface and not every wall, otherwise
the room will look smaller.

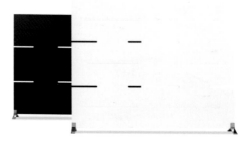

Some paintings, tapestries or murals
can be integrated perfectly in
a principally minimalist space,
so long as the shapes and colors
are soft and subtle.

Lights and Transparencies

Patterns of light and translucent materials in minimalist spaces

In decoration, we often turn to elements made from transparent and translucent materials. This achieves a certain sophisticated look while also enhancing the feeling of space and light. Opaque furniture impedes the passage of light and reduces clarity, as it is an obstacle to it passing. There are many materials that offer a solution to this, thanks to their transparency: glass and plastics like methacrylate and polycarbonate.

These materials are usually found in different furniture items, particularly tables and chairs, as well as in ornaments. But there is also another very common application which affords practical solutions to walls and separations: glass doors or walls. They make it possible to close off a space and insulate it acoustically without losing a broad and general view of the total area. One example is a glass shower wall in the bathroom, which protects the room from splashes without having to resort to cumbersome enclosures. In some homes, the space allocated to the office or study is set apart from other areas using glass walls or doors of a translucent material. For a much more personal style with an original touch, these furniture items or separating elements can be made in different colors.

Light is a great ally in minimalist decoration. Because it uses points of light, bright elements and different combinations, it can create a unique and special space without having to resort to multiple elements. Almost bare spaces become cozy corners with tons of personality if complemented with a careful lighting plan designed specifically for each case. Pale light gives a feeling of space, purity and simplicity, while warmer tones and even colored lights add a more precise touch to any design. It was British mathematician and physicist Sir Isaac Newton who established a basic principle which is still accepted today and which provides the key to this chapter: light is color.

■

The lighting you choose can radically
change the purpose of any decoration.
Colors can be toned down or emphasized
by playing with intensity.

Tinted glass makes it possible to apply
colors to furniture and decorative
elements in a way that matches
the ambiance and adapts to the
delicateness of pure lines.

The transparent nature of some
materials like glass and methacrylate
enable their use in different colors
without obstructing the passage of light.

White light is best for spaces that draw
on a minimalist inspiration, enabling the
room to be appreciated more clearly.

The right arrangement of lighting, both
natural and artificial, noticeably shores
up the color intensity and gives a more
expressive result.

Some materials allow the light to reflect
off them. This effect makes the space
where they are found look much
bigger and brighter.

The glass used in sliding doors or walls
can be tinted different colors to add
a note of color via an essential element.

If tinted glass is used in spaces
dominated by white, the color is
subtly reflected on the walls
and other elements.

Two-Tone

Multiple combinations of two colors

Duality, despite being made up of two distinct elements, can coexist in one state, one person, one object and even one space. The number two is even, considered the perfect union of two different elements that coexist to create a unique combination. To the simplicity and elemental nature of the unit, i.e., the minimum expression, another element is added. In this way, the sobriety of the unit is subtly altered with just one new element, but this small addition can completely change the initial intention of the unit.

In the case of colors, this union can occur in different ways. One of the fundamental principles of the color theory is based on the rule of complementarity. There are three primary colors: red, yellow and blue. Each can be complemented with another color, which is formed by mixing two primaries and which, paradoxically, is found on the opposite side of the color wheel. The complement of a primary, e.g., magenta, is achieved, oddly enough, simply by combining the other two primaries. This reveals

that for two colors to be complementary and to combine well, they do not have to share any of the colors from which they were formed. When this happens, it involves similar colors, whose combination is not very visually attractive and which is usually employed with a particular aesthetic purpose.

That is why, by using only two colors, you can achieve very simple and pure spaces at the decorative level which exude personality and achieve a unique atmosphere. If the colors are complementary, you can achieve a visually pleasant space, regardless of the mixture. The combination of two more subtle and delicate elements is the one that mixes two distinct tones of the same color. The only difference lies in their intensity, and this can be used to achieve a pleasant and harmonious chromatic unity. With the use and suitable choice of colors you can achieve very simple and minimalist spaces that convey a unique character. Contrasts, complementarities, the use of two superimposed bright tones or a play of intensities become the essence of the decoration of minimalist spaces.

Orange and red tones transmit a great
deal of strength, dynamism and vitality,
so their contrast becomes the focal
point of the décor.

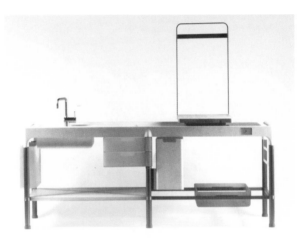

■

Warm touches are the best choice in the
bathroom, where most of the furniture is
made from cold materials like porcelain
and stainless steel.

The contrast from mixing black with
yellow is highly magnetic and quite
masculine in character.

To break away from the sobriety and
elegance of black, there is nothing better
than a touch of orange, one of the
loudest, brightest colors in the palette.

Red and black, like the Stendhal novel
Le Rouge et le Noir, combine in
a unique force, as the sobriety of the
black complements and shores
up the vivacity of the red.

This tandem of cold and fairly dark
colors makes it necessary to turn to
neutral, simple-line decorative elements
to prevent an overly elaborate space.

One subtle way to break with the
chromatic duality without altering its
intention is to seek intermediate tones,
as occurs here with the gray couch.

Red and yellow tones, along with black,
combine perfectly with gray and
metallic details.

The combination of bathroom furniture
in dark tones like wengue and the
orange cabinet top give this decoration
a certain Zen air.

The apple-green color on this bathroom
wall breaks with the sobriety of the dark
timber floor and furniture, while also
adding brightness and dynamism.

The vitality and luminosity of the
mustard color on the back and
armrests of this chair is perfectly
offset against the darker tone of
the rest of the structure.

Although yellow and green are not
complementary, the simple lines of this
corner and the tones chosen enable
the colors to match perfectly.

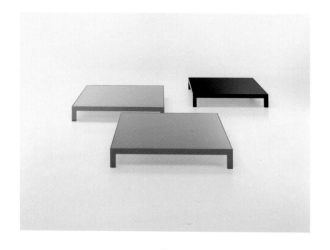

The play of contrasts between
identical pieces of furniture with
different-colored finishes is another way
to add a note of color to the décor.

To decorate minimalist spaces without
renouncing patterns, use designs
with straight lines and gradations
of the same color.

Red bench tops and cupboards make
this kitchen dynamic, while white
prevails to enhance the feeling of space.

The ochre-colored wall is the feature
piece of this dining room, adding
luminosity and warmth, reinforced by
the significant strength of vermilion.

Yellow, ochre and different tones of
brown are colors found in nature, which
is why they can achieve serene,
harmonious spaces.

Although they share no tone, blue and
orange are complementary colors whose
combination gives a pleasant and,
in this case, bright result.

Minimalism does not have to mean no
color. You can maintain its essence
without renouncing the combination of
sober or even dark tones.

Colors like violet and dark brown
combine perfectly with yellows, grays
and blacks, as they complement each
other and create an attractive contrast.

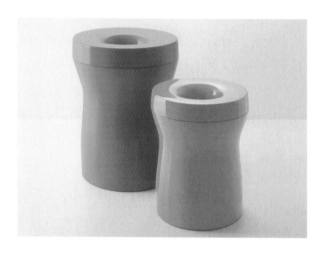

Bathrooms are filled with vitality and
energy through the use of warm, bright
tones like this red, repeated in numerous
details to create an aesthetic harmony.

White and More

Application of color onto pure white

If you want to make a color combination without worrying about losing the purity and simplicity that define the minimalist style, one of the two colors should, without a doubt, be white. Its luminosity will make up for the use of any other color, regardless of how saturated or dark it is. In the space to decorate, the dominant color will of course be the tone that complements white. The latter will be used as the base, as a neutral color that prepares the canvas on which the leading elements are arranged.

According to the tone chosen to complement white, you will manage to convey one sensation or another in the space to decorate. If you use a very toned-down color, a pale shade, with white as well, the final atmosphere will be serene, gentle and very relaxing. On the other hand, if you use a highly saturated and much denser tone it will convey brightness and energy and become the focal point of the décor.

Furniture often becomes the key piece. To keep to the minimalist look, one of the best options is to create a white space where the most basic structures have clear, pure lines, and leave it up to the items of furniture and other ornaments to add a note of color against the pure white. So, in front of a large white wall decorated with a white bookshelf, you could position a red, blue or green couch, for example, to achieve a major contrast and make it the touch of color that completes the decorative project.

It is important to bear in mind that when you combine white with another very bright color, such as yellow, for example, the perception of clarity is multiplied. The space will look like a large source of light. If, on the other hand, you choose a dull color like navy blue, the space will lose its brightness and have a more reserved character.

■

The combination of white and red is a
sure bet in spaces where you want to
achieve a pure, clean ambiance with
a shot of vitality.

With a simple brushstroke of color you
can add personality to designs where
simple lines and a lack of decorative
elements reign.

The harmony and stability that green
gives off is a perfect match for a simple,
bright white background, maintaining
a relaxing balance.

Red adds a great deal of personality to
any space and décor. Its stands out
bright and lively against a neutral
background like white.

The strong point of color dualities is not
that they just suggest each color
separately, but also the effect formed
from their contrast.

La estación del NORTE en VALENCIA. La unión de todas las artes

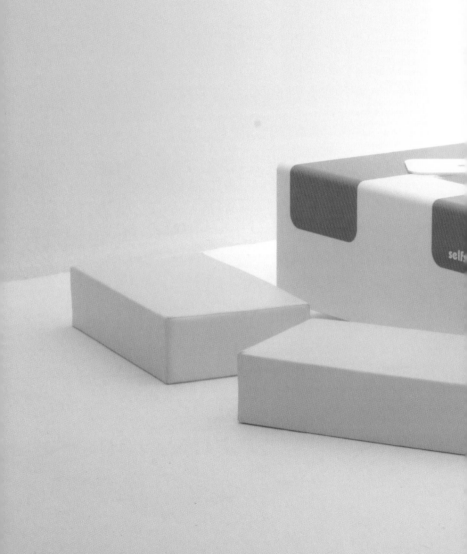

Orange brings a touch of informality
to any design. With a simple detail
in this tone you can combine simplicity
with a casual style.

The contrast between two colors like
white and red perfectly delimits the
entrance zone, in this case the stairs and
the room they lead to.

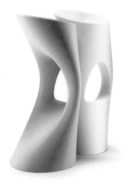

By combining yellow with white you can emphasize the brightness of any element or space, as both colors reflect the light intensely.

In homes with open-plan spaces you can differentiate one specific zone, such as the kitchen, through the use of a color, without having to add more elements.

It is always a good choice to opt for white. Small touches of color can break the monotony, respecting the minimalist style of the shapes.

The softness and freshness that green
gives off makes it the perfect
counterpoint to white in spaces such as
a dining room or kitchen.

This play of colors is one of the
brightest and most lively you can create.
White forms the backdrop for an orange
that transmits dynamism and energy.

The austerity and vacuity of spaces
inspired by minimalism can be
compensated for, to some degree, with
the application of bright colors.

To maintain a feeling of space it is
necessary to simplify lines as much as
possible. The revitalizing effects
of green make it the perfect color for
this type of room.

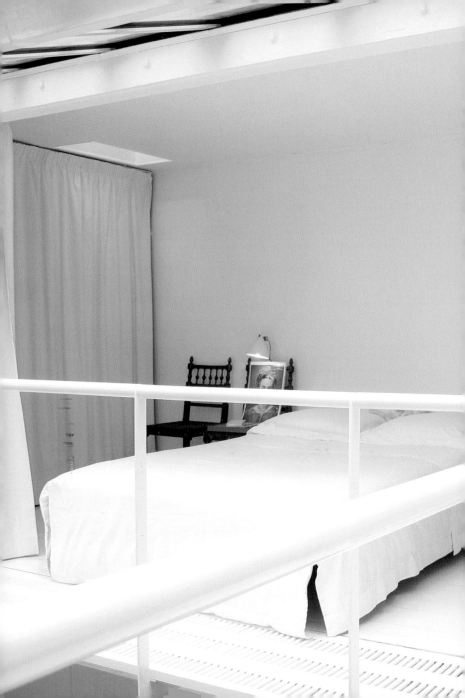

To achieve a simple space without
dispensing with color, one idea is to
select a single contrasting tone and
maintain the pattern.

■

One way of applying color without
changing the rest of the décor is to paint
a single wall a different color, making it
the focal point with respect to the rest
of the snow-white surfaces.

The repeated use of the same color,
in contrast with the background tone
of the room, reinforces the contrasts
achieved by their combination.

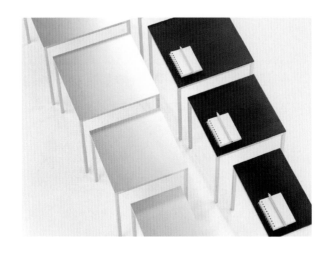

To break away from the sobriety and
neutrality of white spaces, just add a
dash of color which will give the room
a more casual, modern look.

Colorful

Fusion of bright colors and tones

Vitality, energy and vigor are some of the feelings you get when you combine many colors in the same space. Color superposition conveys a great deal of energy and creates a lively look. There is a branch of psychology based on the study of colors and their effects on people. This branch studies the feelings associated with each color when used as a stimulus on people. It is called color psychology and is based on the psychological effects and feelings achieved via distinct colors. However, these feelings can also be derived from cultural factors as, whether consciously or not, some colors are related with particular situations, experiences or cultural episodes.

In spaces where various colors have been mixed that convey diverse emotions and sensations, such as tranquility (achieved with white and pastel shades such as sky blue), strength (red or orange) and motivation (yellow tones), they join up to become an explosive mix that translates into color euphoria. For this reason, it is a good idea to save multiple combinations for areas where it is not necessary to create a peaceful, serene space. It would be completely counterproductive in rooms like bedrooms or living rooms, but on the other hand, it is a very good idea to apply such mixes in game rooms, other rooms allocated to leisure purposes or passageways, as they can activate the imagination and transmit dynamism. It is also common to combine colors in children's bedrooms, to stimulate them and create an energetic and fun world. This achieves a fantasy space, although using too many bright colors could lead to a lack of concentration and hinder full relaxation.

Mixing colors from the same group
enables unlimited play with different
tones, as the resulting color
harmony is assured.

Mixing black with interesting colors like
yellow, green or lime makes for a
younger, more casual ambiance without
renouncing the simplicity of the lines.

■

The play of colors has been applied
directly to the walls, making it possible
to decorate the room with simple,
neutral pieces and without
abandoning color.

Original furniture in unusual shapes
and bright colors can form part of the
minimalist look; some designs combine
them perfectly.

The combination of various colors does
not always have to mean a strident
result, as some compositions can
maintain a clearly minimalist space.

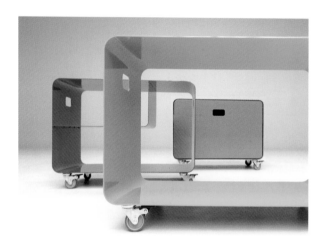

■

The choice of bright colors like red, pink
or orange is always a sure bet in spaces
where you want to convey a happy,
dynamic effect.

Pink has clearly feminine connotations.
Its use in different shades emphasizes
this feeling, although you can still
uphold visual harmony.

By unifying all the surfaces and
furniture under the essence of a single
color, you can accentuate the impact as
it creates color coherence.

■

Black and white always cede
importance to the third color. They
shore up the brightness of red and
convey serenity and relaxation when
used with blue.

Expressive and energetic colors like red
and orange applied generously mean the
other decorative elements should be
kept as neutral and simple as possible.

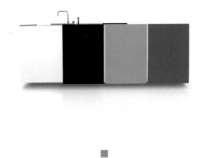

Some colors acquire distinct nuances in
line with the tones they are used with.
Here we see that green, combined
with other neutral colors, shores up the
sober and elegant look of this kitchen.

Orange and blue are complementary
colors and, despite their forceful
presence in this kitchen and
dining room, continue to uphold
a minimalist air.

These simple dressing rooms, open to
the rest of the space, are a decorative
element in themselves thanks to the
bright colors in which they are painted.

The sheets of this sliding panel have
been used as the perfect canvas
for a bright color combination. Once
slid back, only one tone can be seen.

■

When the furniture features simple lines
and the space is big enough, the use
of loud colors with a great deal
of character is no impediment to
a sober style.

Patterned surfaces are hard to reconcile
with a minimalist look. However, if
applied to just one wall they can add
a unique and personal counterpoint.

■

Repeating the same tones in different
elements of a single space shores up the
personality of the design and establishes
a pattern that simplifies its perception.

■

Although minimalism features
a predominance of straight lines, round
shapes can go with the style if you get
the color combination right.

Furniture with finishes in bright, strident
colors stand out against a dark wall,
e.g., black or gray.

Don't refuse to use color out of a fear
of the space losing its austere character:
you can use particular pieces of
furniture to add this expressive touch.

Orange awakens creativity, making it
perfect for children's bedrooms.
Details in gray add a certain necessary
touch of moderation.

Mixing colors with a clear
predominance of tones from the cold
group makes any space relaxing.

Green is a color that invites you to
relax and chill out, and when
combined with brighter colors will
tone down their intensity.

You can complete the decoration of any
space, despite not having much furniture
or only having very simple pieces, just
through the use of colors.

Because of its stimulating effects,
this type of bright color combination is
reserved for areas like the kitchen,
dining room or game room.

Black becomes a key factor in
maintaining a sober aesthetic despite
the application of brightly colored
elements, as it achieves
a certain balance.

With such a marked use of red, no space
remains indifferent. Its powerful
character means the explosion of vitality
invades the whole room.

The use of strident colors always has a
great visual impact, which is why it is
important to apply them in spaces not
designed to wind down in.

Color can be the best tool for a fresh,
fun look without using many different
decorative elements.

In kitchens, the use of citrus colors like
yellow, orange, or even red tones is
associated with particular foods and
at the same time can create
a dynamic ambiance.

In bathrooms with minimalist-style
furniture you can get a different look by
applying colors to the furniture as well
as the walls and floor.

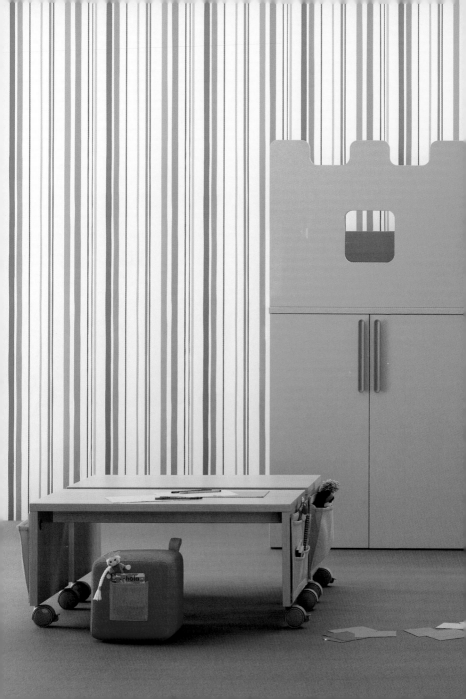

Ethereal Spaces

Careful use of color

Serenity, relaxation and harmony can be conveyed via a suitable and balanced mix of elements, colors and, perhaps most important of all, their intensities. If the aim is to achieve a calm and relaxed atmosphere, as well as cutting the use of furniture to a minimum and using simple, straight shapes, it is necessary to bear the color aspect in mind, as it can be decisive when it comes to achieving a suitable space. To attain ethereal spaces it is necessary to keep a room as empty as possible, eliminating all unnecessary elements and accessories and conserving a general vision of the whole of the space. With this you can achieve the effect of more space, as all extensive and uncluttered areas convey a pleasurable feeling of being able to breathe deeply, and this makes it possible to reach a state of relaxation.

Colors are just as or more important than the right choice of decorative style and furniture. Soft tones transmit serenity and tranquility, reflecting much more light, which reverberates on the surface. Pastel or toned-down shades, achieved by mixing any color with white, mean you don't have to renounce your favorite colors, although they will have to be applied subtly. They can continue to be bright and confer serenity and delicateness on each space, while still revealing their personality before being toned down. For people of a nervous disposition or who find it hard to unwind, this type of space, done up in soft colors, is best, as they stop the senses from being overly excited, even if in an unconscious or passive fashion.

Areas where it is most suitable to choose these types of combinations, with few elements in pale and delicate shades, are rooms used for relaxing in, such as the living room and bedroom. Although the bathroom is a basically functional part of the house, it can also become a relaxation zone, a small home-based spa. Adjustable lights are the best option for complementing spaces allocated for the pleasure of the senses and the relaxation of body and mind.

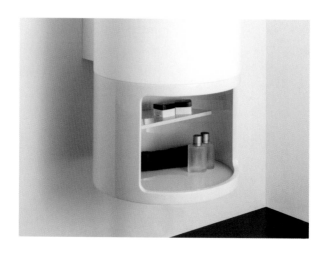

Soft colors like sky blue, as well as providing blue reflections in rooms dominated by white, achieve a really relaxing environment.

Earthy tones combined with soft, warm
colors make for a comfortable and
welcoming space, even when a number of
metallic details or mirrors are added.

You can achieve a minimalist and light
decoration with some patterns,
particularly ones with straight lines
in pale, luminous colors.

Applying a soft tone like this blue to
a background with harder colors like
black can lessen its coldness and turn
any space into a pleasant corner.

The application of a number of color
details such as the yellow wall and sky-
blue bench tops breaks with the coldness
of steel and white without renouncing
the feeling of delicateness.

■

For a really light and minimalist
ambiance, go for large, empty spaces
with a clear predominance of white.

Character is basically defined by shades,
which determine the force and
purpose of the chosen tone as well as
the feelings it conveys.

Austerity is one of the main features of
minimalism. To break away from
its neutrality, you only need a dash
of a soft color that respects its
lightness and harmony.

The purity and simplicity of the décor is
not lost with the use of various colors.
Everything depends on their intensity
and the mix chosen.

To add a touch of warmth and even
a rustic look to any ambiance without
losing its modern, contemporary feel,
one good idea is to paint wooden
furniture a different color.

Keeping furniture down to a few
carefully chosen basic pieces can help
create relaxed, peaceful environments,
particularly for rooms like studies
or home offices.

The freshness of green against a
predominantly white background shores
up the idea of delicateness and fragility
that characterizes ethereal spaces.

Lighting is a crucial factor in the design
of any space. If there is plenty of light
you can use darker tones
without worrying the result will be
too sober or dull.

For reading or meeting areas,
prominence can be given to key furniture
pieces such as chairs or tables,
reaffirming the use for which
the area is allocated.

White makes it possible to make the
most of the natural light in any space,
as it is the tone that reflects it the most,
giving a heightened feeling of space.

In areas with a predominance of neutral
colors like white, beige or black,
details in bright colors complement
the design and respect the soft, relaxed
esthetic at the same time.

Spaces earmarked for work require
a pleasant, calm environment. White can
help lift your concentration thanks to
its absolute neutrality.

■

The application of bright colors in some
pieces of furniture or decorative
ornaments can coexist perfectly with the
design of a serene space.

To design a space that radiates a feeling
of amplitude and well being, one of the
best recourses is to apply white, which
exudes purity and brightness.

If the walls and ceiling are dark, the
choice of pure white furniture and some
decorative elements will provide
a pleasant contrast.

One of the properties of olive green is
that it translates the values of
spirituality into daily life, as well as
a harmony which reaches its zenith
when paired with white.

Pastel colors, i.e., ones that have been
toned down by adding white, suggest
softness and delicacy and are perfect for
recreating placid environments.

Choice of materials and their
combination is another key factor,
as they can also determine the overall
perception of the designed space.

Colors like blue and green usually
convey coldness. However, if applied
as touches of color to a neutral room,
they add personality without breaking
the harmony.

■

The freshness of colors related with
nature, such as wood brown or green,
create welcoming, serene environments.

For the kitchen to transmit a feeling of
space, bright colors are reserved
for some of the corners and furniture,
while the rest is kept in neutral,
bright tones.

Wood colors exude a feeling of warmth
and protection. Combining them
with pure line designer furniture means
the space conveys a sense of peace.

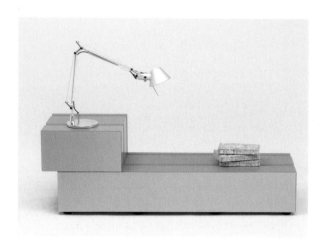

Colors like pink or mauve, despite their
bright character, add a touch of delicacy
and femininity which reinforces the aim
of creating a serene and relaxed space.

ART NOW

Betting on a combination of white, black
and gray is always going to be
successful if the idea is to create
a peaceful, pleasant and, above all,
neutral space.

Just a Warm Touch

Spaces that confer warmth through color

The division between warm and cold colors is based solely on human perception and experiences and theories that have arisen around the topic throughout history. Warm colors range from yellow to red and include orange, vermilion and all those colors in between. This differentiation with respect to cold colors (basically blues and greens) is mostly based on the behavior of light with each one, and the sensory and psychological perception they exude. Warmth and coldness are thermal feelings. The sun is perceived as being yellow, even orange at sundown, and is related with the heat these colors exude, which are also more adept at capturing light. The same thing happens with flames, which are perceived as being orange with yellow tones. For that reason, together with other less evident or associative factors, these colors are considered to be in the warm range. In short, the warm range is formed of yellow, orange, red and pink, although some violets with red pigments and warm colors in lighter shades, such as cream colors, can also be considered

warm. They all suggest hospitality, warmth, delicateness and kindness, and are associated with the warmer and more flower-filled seasons, i.e., spring and summer. Also, they transmit the vitality of the sun and inspire vigor and dynamism, while also toning and stimulating.

There are other intermediate tones where a cold color has been combined with a touch of a warm tone or vice-versa. In these cases, it is possible that a cold color to which a bit of warmth has been added inclines more toward the warm range, and as a result the mix is perceived along this line. That is why it is sometimes hard to draw a clear line, as simple shades can tip the scale one way or the other.

In decoration, each warm color is associated with a very particular purpose. Yellow, although not very saturated, is perfect for relaxation and study, as is green. They can be used in bedrooms, offices and studies. Pink suggests femininity and delicateness, while red, for example, is pure force, energy and intensity.

A good way to tone down the coldness of
a bathroom is to add a touch of warmth
through colors like this bright orange.

The use of colors from the warm range
makes it possible to create welcoming,
comfortable spaces without having
to employ more decorative elements
or accessories.

A Consommer sans modération

Saint Jacques poelées
- 20 noix de S' Jacque
- 2 feuilles de brick
- 40 gr Mesclun
- 4 brins de cerfeuil et ciboulette
- 2 cuil à soupe de sirop d'érable
- 20 g de beurre

Risotto à la trévise
- 400g riz carnaroli
- 1 kg de Trévise
- 3 bouillons de volaille
- 1 oignon
- 10cl d'huile d'olive
- 15cl de vin blanc
- 80g de parmesan
- 80 g de beurre.

Soufflé au conté
- 30 cl de lait
- 4 oeufs
- 30 g de farine
- 100 g de conté rapé
- 60 g de beurre
- 1 pincée Noix de
- Muscade

Cheese Cake
- 600g St Moret
- 4 oeufs
- 100 g de Sucre Maizena
- 1 sct à soupe Maizena
- 3 fruits de la passion
- 120g biscuits à la cannelle.

Although green is usually considered
a cold color, its shades can ensure
it transmits a certain level of warmth
and luminosity.

Simple lines in the kitchen and dining
room, which help achieve a large
and functional space, can be
complemented with bright colors
that personalize the space.

In kitchens with straight lines and cold
materials like steel, lime will break up
the sobriety and add a strident touch.

In spaces dominated by a palette of
dark, dull colors, red becomes a focus
point and harmonious counterpoint
at the same time.

The big advantage of warm colors is
that with just one detail you can add
personality to any space without having
to have a multitude of elements.

Brown is one of the most neutral colors
in the palette. Its shades make it a
perfect color for pleasant, serene
ambiances, regardless of the shade
of brown used.

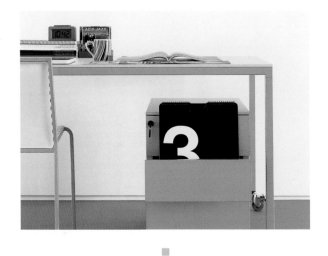

To compensate for the search for the
essential, which is the basis on which
minimalism is grounded, you can
turn to the strength and brightness of
red or orange, colors with a great
deal of personality.

The convincing use of a single color
makes it possible to opt for simple,
neutral furniture, as all the attention
will be on the walls—in this case
a stimulating and energetic lime color.

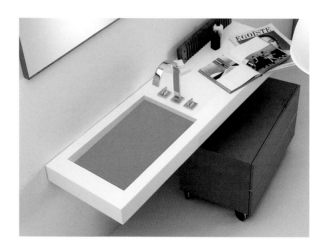

■

Pink tones and fuchsia in particular
give a casual look to any décor and
convey a daring take on femininity.

■

To achieve a modern, minimalist look
with character, there is one trio that
never fails: the combination of white,
black and a few notes of red.

The strength of orange applied to just
two pieces of furniture turns this
completely neutral bright white space
into a corner with plenty of personality.

Although red is not commonly used in studies and home offices, it is a tone that conveys the right vitality and energy for work.

When you have a large space ruled by
white, small touches of color break
the sober monochrome feeling.

The combination of warm elements such
as the type of lighting or the colors of
the walls and furniture achieve a much
cozier effect.

In contrast with the rustic look of the
walls and floors, the modern lines
of the furniture and the bright colors
stand out with respect to the rest.

The red surface that covers the kitchen
wall has a reflective property that
reverberates with the light and permits
increased luminosity in the work space.

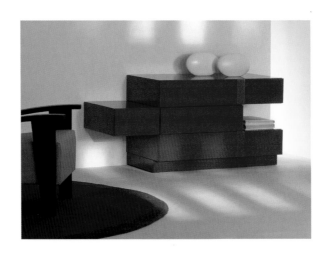

With simple red furniture you can
change a small corner of the room into
a space that invites sociability
and dynamism.

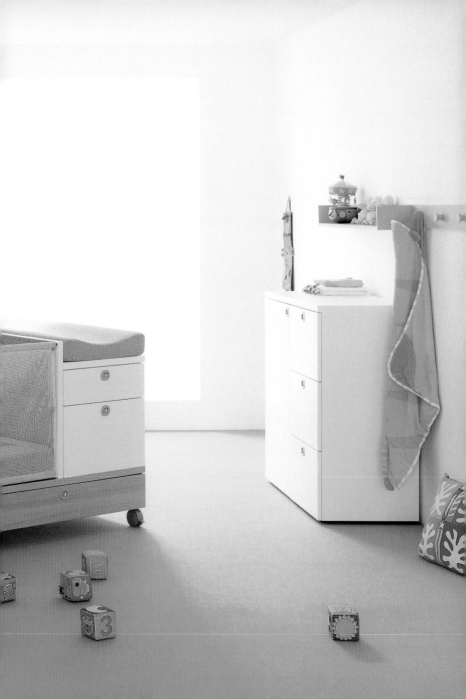

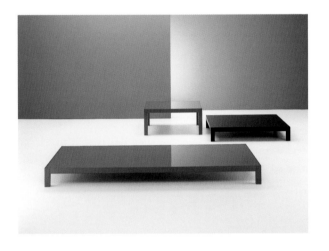

Despite the soberness that black
impregnates in any space, the presence
of red manages to completely eradicate
this feeling and adds vitality.

■

With just a touch of color and certain
pieces of strategically positioned
furniture like armchairs and
couches you get a totally different
and personal space.

Just a Cold Touch

Subdued and serene spaces with cool colors

The direction of a thing often lies in the detail and purpose. In the case of colors, this responsibility falls fundamentally on shades, as they define what type of space and what feelings are achieved, depending on the shade chosen. Cold colors with cold shades express freshness, serenity, calm, delicateness, rest, peace and hope. On the other hand, colors in dark shades with a predominance of blue are associated with mystery and melancholy. Cold colors are green, blue and violet, lavender and gray. They are mainly associated with water and metals, i.e., elements that are cold by nature. They are great for concentration, rest and relaxation, and to recreate fresh and serene spaces.

In decoration, cold tones with light shades are best for rooms destined for relaxation. Light blues and greens or pastel shades contribute the serenity needed. It is also common to find these touches of color in the bathroom. This is the water zone *par excellence* and is associated with purity and freshness. Blues and greens, or aquamarines, imitate the color of water, recreating a harmonious and sensorial space.

However, they are very delicate colors when it comes to designing a space. As occurs with the warm colors, if the purpose is to achieve a minimalist ambiance, free of excesses and seeking simplification, it is preferable to opt for small touches, such as in some items of furniture, or accessories and ornaments. This will help keep the rest of the space light and bright, avoiding elements that darken it and make it seem smaller. Objects painted or finished in these colors will always look much smaller and appear further away than those with warm tones. In this case it is also necessary to bear in mind other colorless elements that transmit the same feeling as cold colors, i.e., mirrors, which are cold by nature and simply reflect what is in the room. If you choose cold colors for decorating a room, it is best to use as few mirrors as possible.

For coffee tables, sideboards in
passageways, couches and even
wardrobes, green, although bright, will
always harmonize and add balance.

Some details in a blue or turquoise
color in the bathroom add freshness
and serenity. It is a tone that stands
out for its delicate and sweet nature
in pale shades.

Turquoise is a color that conveys fluidity
and makes any space breathe a pleasant
atmosphere. Its shades mean that,
together with white, it contributes
a great deal of brightness.

As well as its happy, fresh character,
green radiates a feeling of balance,
meaning that a dash of it in neutral
spaces will enhance the design harmony.

■

Despite its bright tone, apple green
creates a very special feeling in living
rooms and other relaxation zones,
as well as a pleasing, balanced contrast.

The colors that form part of the cold
range do not always transmit a feeling
of hardness and coldness; it depends
on their application and combination
in each case.

Sometimes colors like blue, green,
turquoise or aquamarine can be used to
break the neutrality of a space, while
still maintaining its sobriety.

Spaces with metallic details and a
predominance of white will find
a perfect counterpoint in green,
as it adds a note of color while
respecting harmony.

■

Some dark blues can add a subtle
color variety to any décor, while the dull
tone maintains the discretion
of the overall look.

■

Apple green can sometimes be perceived
as a warm tone, as it stands out
among cold materials like steel,
glass or porcelain.

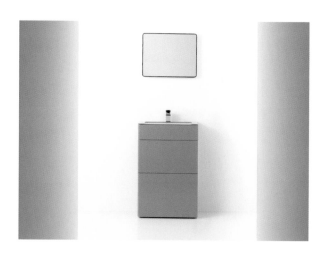

The effect of this color range is
multiplied if it is used in some details,
while the rest of the elements are kept
in completely neutral colors.

■

Sometimes the perception of a space as
warm or cold does not even depend on
the colors that have been applied, but
rather the result of how they were mixed
and the purpose.

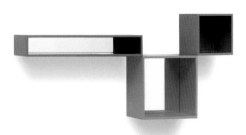

■

Just a few small details like a bookshelf
or other decorative ornaments are
enough for these tones to convey their
personality to the whole look and
modify its perception.

Balance, serenity and relaxation define
the color green, which is why it is
appropriate for spaces like bedrooms
and studies, as it is both motivating
and calming.

Despite the subtle presence of a few
elements in cold colors, it is practically
impossible not to notice the effects
they have on the décor.

One good way to make the most of the
qualities of these colors, such as green
in all its shades, is to make them into
the feature pieces of the room against
other neutral colors.

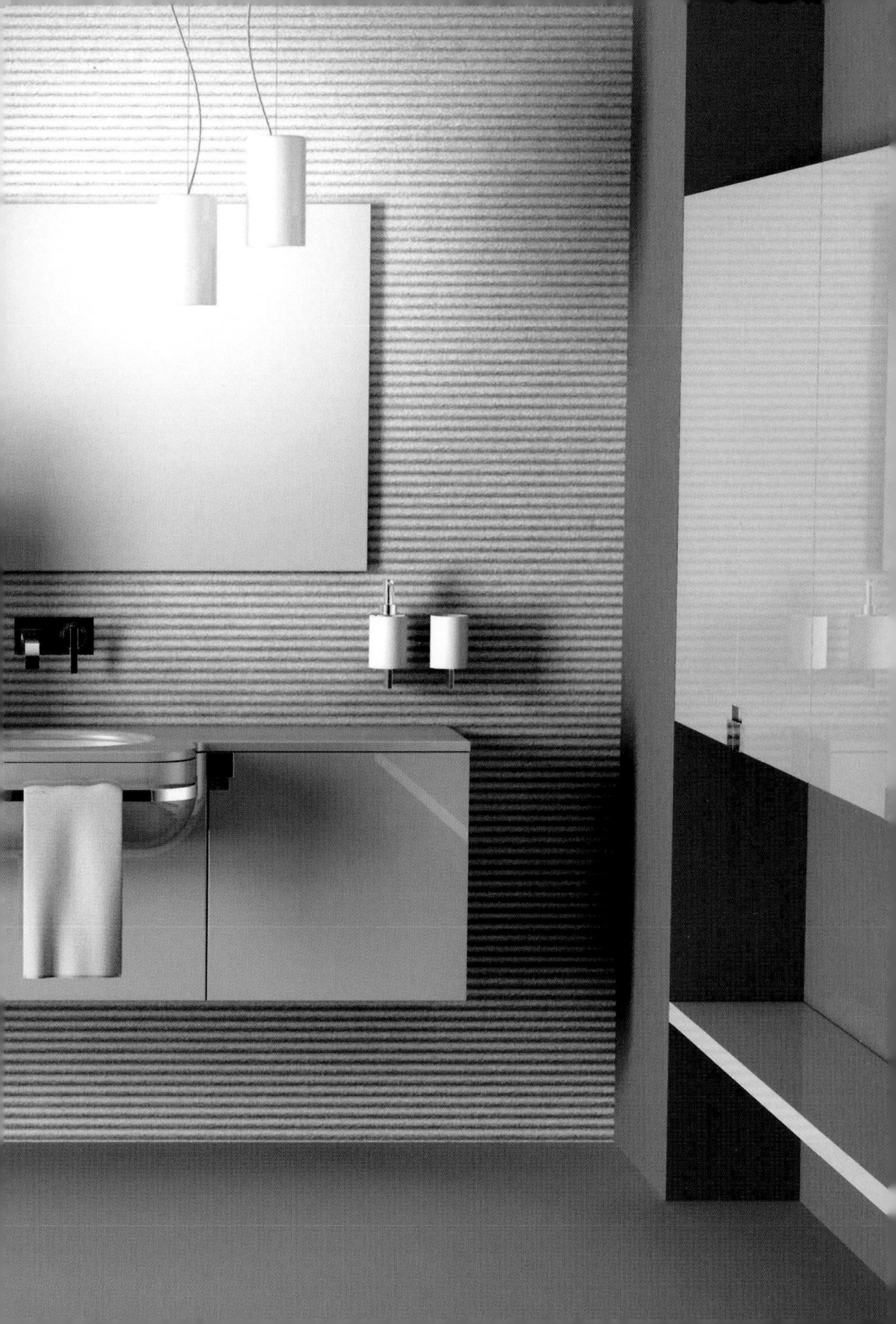

Manufacturers

ABR
Córcega 195-197, interior
08036 Barcelona, Spain
P: +34 93 363 72 92
info@abrproduccion.com
www.abrproduccion.com

Bonn
Coffee table designed by Toni Pallejà
(Porcuatro)
White, black, yellow, blue and orange

Agape
Via Po Barna 69
46031 Correggio Micheli di Bagnolo San Vito (MN), Italy
P: +39 376 250 311
info@agapedesign.it
www.agapedesign.it

4x4
Wall mirror designed by Benedini
Associati (Bibi, Camila, Giampaolo
Benedini)
White, gray, green and orange

4x4
Wall lamp designed by Benedini
Associati (Bibi, Camila, Giampaolo
Benedini)
White, gray, green and orange

Carrara

Marble sink
White Carrara marble

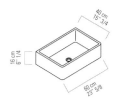

Deep

Bathtub designed by Benedini
Associati (Bibi, Camila, Giampaolo
Benedini)
White

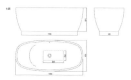

Roto

Wastepaper bin and basket designed
by M. Negri and Benedini Associati
(Bibi, Camila, Giampaolo Benedini)
Orange, green, white and gray

Alivar
Via L. Da Vinci 118/14
50028 Tavarnelle Val di Pesa (FI), Italy
P: +39 558 070 115
alivar@alivar.com
www.alivar.com

Buddy Boss

Armchair upholstered in fabric or
leather designed by Bruno Rainaldi
White, orange and other colors

art. 9241
L/W 71   H 75   P/D 65
W 28"   H 29,5"   D 25,6"

Buddy Boss

Sofa upholstered in fabric or leather
designed by Bruno Rainaldi
White, orange and other colors

art. 9242
L/W 127   H 75   P/D 65
W 50"   H 29,5"   D 25,6"

Altro

La Coma 18, A1 Pol. Ind. Pla de Santa Ana
08272 St. Fruitós de Bages, Barcelona, Spain
P: +34 93 878 98 90
altro@altro.es
www.altro.es

Box

Cabinet and ceramic WC set from
the Altro collection
White, gray, green, maroon and other
colors

Name

Structure formed of towel rack and
sink top
Silver metal, marble or glass

Antonio Lupi

Via Mazzini 73/75
50050 Stabbia, Cerreto Guidi (FI), Italy
P: +39 571 586 881
lupi@antoniolupi.it
www.antoniolupi.it

Bella

Bathtub designed by Carlo Colombo
White or with the external part
lacquered in a color in the range

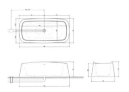

Tuga

Collection designed by Studio
Carlesi Design
White, orange, green, pink, blue, red
and other colors

Apavisa
Ctra. Castellón-San Juan de Moró Km 0,75
12130 San Juan de Moró, Castellón, Spain
P: +34 96 470 11 20
info@apavisa.com
www.apavisa.com

Arflex
Viale Monza 17
20034 Giussano (MI), Italy
P: +39 362 853 043
info@arflex.it
www.arflex.it

Aura

Chair with ebony or finishes
or leather upholstery designed by
Carlo Colombo
White, black and various tones of
brown or ebony wood

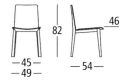

Bagutta

Writing desk designed by Annig
Sarian
White and black

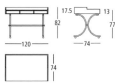

Cubotto

Black or white minibar in MDF
designed by Cini Boeri
Black and white

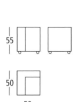

Elettra

Tubular structure armchair in chrome
or black designed by BBPR
Blue, white, black and every color in
the range

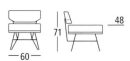

Femme

Sofa and armchair designed by
Carlo Colombo
Red, brown, lilac and many other
colors in the range

240

Martingala

Armchair designed by Marco Zanuso
White, brown, red and every color in
the range

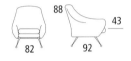

88

43

82

92

Arketipo
Via Garibaldi 72
50041 Calenzano (FI), Italy
P: +39 558 876 248/558 877 212
info@arketipo.com
www.arketipo.com

Kono

Swivel armchair designed by Carlo
Bimbi
White and black

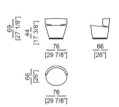

69
[27 1/8"]

44
[17 3/8"]

76
[29 7/8"]

66
[26"]

66
[26"]

76
[29 7/8"]

Must

Sofa designed by Carlo Bimbi and
Adriano Piazzesi
White

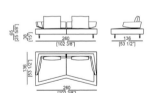

65
[25 5/8"]

38
[15"]

260
[102 3/8"]

136
[53 1/2"]

136
[53 1/2"]

260
[102 3/8"]

Artificio

Padilla 31
28006 Madrid, Spain
P: +34 91 533 40 40
comunicacion@artificio.es
www.artificio.es

Compacta
Kitchen island
Combination of colors in white, black, gray and green

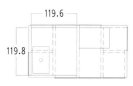

Artifort

Lande Productie Schijndel B.V., PO Box 115 – NL 5480 AC Schijndel
Van Leeuwenhoekweg 20 5482 TK Schijndel, The Netherlands
P: +31 73 658 00 20
info@artifort.com
www.artifort.com

F 598
Armchair designed by Pierre Paulin
Orange, blue, red and other colors

Kirk
Metal structure armchair with tubular base designed by René Holten
Green, red, white and other colors and combinations

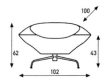

Lilla
Stool designed by Patrick Norguet
Blue, green, orange and other colors

Axia

Via del Credito 183
1033 Castelfranco Veneto (TV), Italy
P: +39 423 496 222
axia@axiabath.it
www.axiabath.it

B&B Italia

B&B Italia USA INC
150 East 58th Street, New York, NY 10155, USA
P: +1 800 872 1697
inof@bebitalia.it
www.bebitalia.it

Lazy pla 57
Collection of chairs and small
armchairs designed by Patricia
Urquiola
Yellow, red, orange and other colors

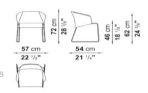

72 cm
28 ³/₈"

57 cm
22 ¹/₂"

54 cm
21 ¹/₄"

46 cm
18 ¹/₈"

62 cm
24 ³/₈"

Lazy pla 80

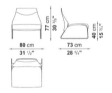

77 cm
30 ¹/₂"

80 cm
31 ¹/₂"

73 cm
28 ³/₄"

40 cm
15 ³/₄"

Lazy pla 77

77 cm
30 ³/₈"

47 cm
18 ¹/₂"

42 cm
16 ¹/₂"

48 cm
18 ¹/₈"

Belligotti

Via Macerata 5
61020 Mentecchio di S. Angelo in Lizzola (PU), Italy
P: +39 721 498 615
belligotti@belligotti.com
www.belligotti.com

Bisazza North America
3540 NW 72nd Avenue
Miami, FL 33122, USA
P: +1 305 597 4099
info@bisazzausa.com
www.bisazzausa.com

Blå Station AB
Box 100 S-296 22
Sandbakteragatan 17, Åhus, Sweden
P: +46 44 249 070
info@blastation.se
www.blastation.se

Fatback
Easy-to-assemble sofa-style
armchairs designed by Fredrik
Mattsson
Black, white, red and other colors
and patterns

Peek Low
Chair with tubular steel feet designed
by Stefan Borselius
Black combined with blue, maroon or
other colors

Snooze Rock
Armchair designed by Stefan
Borselius and Fredrik Mattsson
Yellow, orange, black and other
colors

Bm2000

Ctra. N-340 Km 1.045, 200 nº 82
12580 Benicarló, Castellón, Spain
P: +34 96 446 73 20
bm2000@bm2000.net
www.bm2000.net

Collection Top Junior 27

BMood

Via G. Fattori 57
42044 Gualtieri (RE), Italy
P: +39 522 829 693
info@bmood.it
www.bmood.it

Degree
Collection characterized by the swivel
movement of its pieces
White, black, orange, yellow and
other colors

Boconcept España S.A.

C.C. Parquesur
28916 Leganés, Madrid, Spain
P: +34 902 225 005
boconcept@boconcept.es
www.boconcept.es

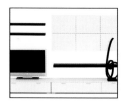

Modii y Occa
White lacquered storage systems
and wall shelving
Black and white

Bonaldo SpA
Via Straelle 3
35010 Villanova (PD), Italy
P: +39 499 299 011
bonaldo@bonaldo.it
www.bonaldo.it

Line

Chair that transforms into chaise
longue designed by Stefan Heiliger
Various colors in fabric or leather

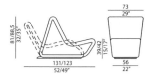

Orbit

Bookshelf with fixed or swivel base
designed by Gino Carollo
Various colors

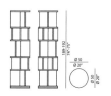

Poly

Stackable polycarbonate chair
designed by Karim Rashid
Transparent, white, black, pink and
other colors

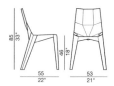

Burgbad
Bad Fredeburg
Kirchplatz 10
57392 Schmallenberg, Germany
P: +49 2974 9617
info@burgbad.de
www.burgbad.de

Accura

Bathroom furniture module with
wheels
White, red, gray and other colors

Casamania

Via S. Elena 3
31040 Signoressa di Trevignano (TV), Italy
P: +39 423 6753
info@casamania.it
www.casamania.it

Koon

Ashtray/wastepaper bin designed by
Karim Rashid
Gray, blue, green, pink, black and
other colors

Cassina

Via Brusneli 1
20036 Meda (MI), Italy
P: +39 362 3721
info@cassina.it
www.cassina.it

Flat

Sideboard designed by Piero Lissoni
White, gray, brown, red and black

Cattelan Italia

Via Pilastri 15
36010 Carrè (VI), Italy
P: +39 445 318 711
info@cattelanitalia.com
www.cattelanitalia.com

Elan

Extending table designed by Paolo
Cattelan
Uncolored or tinted glass with metal
or leather-clad legs

Monaco Inox

Table designed by Giorgio Cattelan
Top in glass, wengue, walnut or
Carrara white marble

Wally

Modular bookshelf designed by Philip
Jackson
White, black or red

Cazaña Design

Av. de Humanes 138, esquina calle Uruguay
28971 Griñón, Madrid, Spain
P: +34 91 814 99 21
www.tc-design.com

Composit

Strada Provinciale Fogliense 41
61020 Montecchio (PS), Italy
P: +39 721 90 971
info@composit.it
www.composit.it

D'dimension

Curbstone AB, Cirkelgatan 26
SE-904 21 Umeå, Sweden
P: +46 768 490 792
info@ddimension.com
www.ddimension.com

D'shelf

Hanging shelf designed by Johan
Sandström
Shiny or matte black or white

Desalto
Via per Montesolaro
22063 Cantù (CO), Italy
P: +39 317 832 211
info@desalto.it
www.desalto.it

A1
Armchair with flat steel profile finished
in chrome designed by Arik Levy
Various colors and combinations

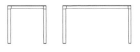

Helsinki XL
Extra-wide table designed by Caronni
& Bonamoni
Chrome, white, black, red and gray

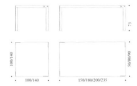

Liko
Table with steel legs and glass tops
designed by Arik Levy
Red, black, white and other colors or
in wood

Sand Air
Light, stackable chair designed by
Pocci & Dondoli
Red, white, gray and other colors

52,5 x 58 x 76 cm

Trace
Original chair designed by Shin
Azumi
White, red and black

528

Desideri Srl
Via A. Durante 49
33080 Prata di Pordeone (PN), Italy
P: +39 434 610 773
info@desiderilineabagno.it
www.desiderilineaebagno.it

Maxim
Washbasin and semi-circular furniture
module
Pink, mustard, black and other colors

Duravit
Pol. Ind. Sector Z, Lógistica 18
08150 Parets del Vallès, Barcelona, Spain
P: +34 902 387 700
info@es.duravit.com
www.duravit.es

Emmebi
Via C. Monteverdi 28
20031 Cesano Maderno (MI), Italy
P: +39 362 502 296
info@emmebidesign.com
www.emmebidesign.com

Brera
Bookshelf available in multiple
dimensions and finishes, designed
by Lievore Altherr Molina
Matte lacquer in 24 colors, wengue,
walnut and ebony

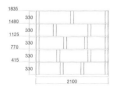

Seventy Day
Multiple combination container
system designed by Pietro Arosio
Matte and shine finish in multiple
colors, wengue, walnut and ebony

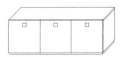

H. 635
W.1800

Engelbrechts
Skindergade 38
DK-1159 Copenhagen K, Denmark
P: +45 3391 9896
info@engelbrechts.com
www.engelbrechts.com

Chairik
Chair made from shaped plywood
Black, yellow, blue and other colors

125
H78,7 x SH45,5 x D55 x W65,5 cm

Plasma
Chair with detachable armrests and
separate back and seat
White, green, orange, red and other
colors

Estudi Hac
Paseo Germanias 12, derecha
46870 Ontinyent, Valencia, Spain
P: +34 96 238 93 40
estudihac@estudihac.com
www.estudihac.com

JPN
Collection of metal-structure furniture
and colored epoxy paint
White, black, red and green

Ring
Round WC designed by Vasic-Home
White

Fratelli Rossetto
Via Principe Umberto
33080 Puja de Prata (PN), Italy
P: +39 434 621 620
info@fratellirossetto.it
www.fratellirossetto.it

Zero Tre Program

Fritz Hansen A/S
Allerød, Denmark
P: +45 4817 2300
mail@fritzhansen.com
www.fritzhansen.com

3208
Chair designed by Arne Jacobsen
White, black and red

Attitude
Easy chair designed by Morten Voss
Orange, green, white, black and
other colors

MV 10

Attitude
Coffee table designed by Morten
Voss
White surface and gray base

Lissoni Lounge Collection
Low Chair
Armchair designed by Piero Lissoni
Black, white and many other colors

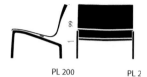

PL 200   PL 2

Space Lounge Chair
Easy chair with plastic seat,
upholstered in fabric or leather and
designed by Jesh & Laub
Black, white or silver base and
upholstery in various colors

The Egg
Reclinable armchair with base in four
points designed by Arne Jacobsen
Red, brown, gray and other colors

Grantour
IPE Cavalli
Via Mattei 1
40069 Zola Predosa (BO), Italy
P: +39 516 186 322
ipe@ipe.it
www.ipe.it

Grup Gamma S.A.
Pol. Ind. Illa Sud 65
08650 Sallent, Barcelona, Spain
P: +34 902 212 170
gamma@gamma.es
www.gamma.es

Cool
Bathroom furniture
Blue, orange, green, white and many
other colors

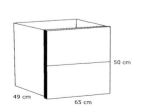

50 cm

49 cm   65 cm

Ibo
Ceramic WC

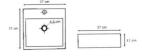

Open
Bathroom cabinet
Wood or lacquered white

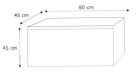

45 cm   60 cm

45 cm

Gubi
Frihavnen, Klubiensvej 7-9, Pakhus 53
2100 Copenhagen, Denmark
P: +45 3332 6368
gubi@gubi.dk
www.gubi.dk

Gubi
Chair designed by Komplot
Yellow, black, red, white and other
colors

83 cm

54 cm

Häcker Küchen GmbH & Co KG
Werkstraße 3
32289 Rödinghausen, Germany
P: +49 5746 9400
info@haecker-kuechen.de
www.haecker-kuechen.de

SM 4030
Kitchen furniture
High-shine gray stone

Hardy Inside
HRD Route de Saint-Malo
CS 26822 35768 Saint-Gregoire Cedex, France
P: +33 223 468 694
info@hardy-roux.com
www.hardyinside.com

Inbani
Ctra. de Ocaña 39
Esc. 2, 1º, planta 1
03007 Alicante, Valencia, Spain
P: +34 96 510 64 65
inbani@inbani.com
www.inbani.com

Ela
Bathroom furniture designed by
Francesc Rifé
Wood, white, green, blue and other
colors

Siluet
Bathroom furniture
Wood, orange, white and other
colors

Strato
Modular bathroom furniture with fine
decorative lines separating the
various modules
Wood, white, blue and other colors

Tambo
Integrated cylindrical-shaped WC and
bathroom cabinet designed by
Sergio Rochas
White washbasin and wood or
various colored furniture pieces

Klaessons AB

PO Box 340
Ydrevägen 23
SE-573 24 Tranås, Sweden
P: +46 140 385 600
info@materia.se
www.materia.se

Adam
Stackable, easy-to-assemble chair
designed by Simo Heikkilä and Yrjö
Wiherheimo
White, black, red, blue and other
colors

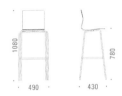

Avec sofa
Sofa bed with folding ends designed
by Birgitta Kööf
In fabric to choose from in various
colors and patterns

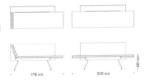

Flok table
Workbench designed by Simo
Heikkilä and Yrjö Wiherheimo
Birch plywood

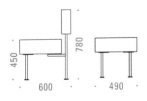

Longo
Sofa, bench and table designed by
Komplot
White, blue, black and other colors
and combinations

May flower
Stackable, easy-to-assemble chair
designed by Lars Pettersson and
Thomas Bernstrand
White, black, gray or lime

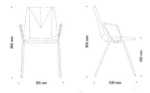

Kohler Co.
444 Highland Drive
Kohler, WI 53044
Wisconsin, USA
P: +1 800 456 4537
www.kohler.com

Purist Hatbox Toilet
Oval WC
Gray, white, black and other colors

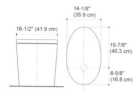

Kristalia Srl
Via Calderano 5
33 070 Brugnera (PN), Italy
P: +39 434 623 678
info@kristalia.it
www.kristalia.it

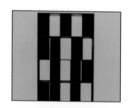

915
Bookshelf in MDF designed by Bartoli
Design
Lacquered, white or black, texturized

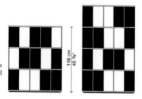

All
Sideboard designed by Bartoli
Design
Wengue wood, dyed gray or with
white, red or gray lacquer

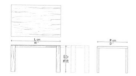

Fifty
Table designed by Ruggero Magrini
& Bluezone
Wood or lacquered in various colors

Oops

Fixed or extending round table
designed by Monica Graffeo
Wengue dyed oak or white or black
lacquer

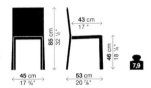

Slim

Metal structure chair with leather
cover designed by Bluezone
Black, red, gray and many other
colors

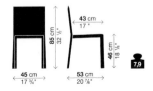

Kundalini

Via F. de Sanctis 34
20141 Milan, Italy
P: +39 236 538 950
info@kundalini.it
www.kundalini.it

Sculptural bench handmade in
lacquered fiberglass designed by
Brodie Neill
Gray, orange, red and black

42x185x56

Lema

Strada Statale Briantea 2, Alzate Brianza
2240 Como, Italy
P: +39 316 30 990
lema@lemamobili.com
www.lemamobili.com

Materia Klaessons AB
PO Box 340
Ydrevägen 23
SE-573 24 Tranås, Sweden
P: +46 140 385 600
info@materia.se
www.materia.se

Bönan

Barstool designed by Sandin
& Bülow
Green, orange, red, black and many
other colors

0605 - 0610

Centrum

Chair designed by Sandin & Bülow
Black, orange, blue and many other
colors

Cosmo

Coffee table with double top in
multiple sizes and shapes designed
by Box Design
White lacquer and oak or birch
plywood

2007
Ø 700 mm
H: 380 / 500 mm

Element

Armchair with armrests designed by
Sandin & Bülow
Many colors in fabric or leather

Giro

Armchair designed by Sandin
& Bülow
Green, black, yellow, white and many
other colors

4911 - 4921

Minimal

Sofa designed by Sandin & Bülow
White, green, brown and many other
colors

S225-H
WxD: 1490 x 730 mm

S225-V
WxD: 1490 x 730 mm

Monolite

Armchair designed by Sandin
& Bülow
Red, green, black and other colors

6111
WxD: 680 x 640 mm
Weight: 24 kg

Obi conference

Table allowing multiple variations
designed by Sandin & Bülow
Glass, oak or birch plywood tabletop

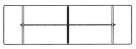

1775
Bredd/Width/Breite 4000 mm
Djup/Depth/Tiefe 1170 mm
Höjd/Height/Höhe 720 mm

Plektrum

Stool designed by Sandin & Bülow
Black, dark crimson and many other
colors

Praline noir

Bench designed by Fredrik Kjellgren
Black and gray

Vågspel

Magazine rack designed by Sandin
& Bülow
Front made from beech, birch or oak
with white, gray or black bottom

MDF Italia SpA
Via Morimondo 5/7
20143 Milan, Italy
P: +39 281 804 100
infomdf@mdfitalia.it
www.mdfitalia.it

Allen
Sofa and armchair with wood
and steel structure designed by
B. Fattorini
Orange, red, gray and many other
colors

288
sed

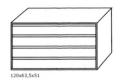

Aluminum Cabinets
Storage systems with doors or
drawers designed by B. Fattorini
White, black, red, gray or orange

120x63,5x51

Arj
Chair with or without wheels,
designed by B. Fattorini
Green, white and other colors

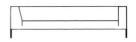

Box
Stackable, swivel module designed
by James Irvine
White

Eleen
Bed with extending headboard
designed by Soda Designers
(Nasrallah and Horner)
Orange, green, black and many other
colors

Erman

Minimalist sofa designed by
B. Fattorini
Yellow, orange, red and many other
colors

255x89xl
seduta 4

Fu 09

Armchair designed by For Use
Structure in white and upholstery in
different colors

La grand table

Aluminum structure table designed
by X. Lust
Aluminum, lacquered aluminum or
matte white

Lofty

Chaise longue with steel structure
and base designed by P. Cazzaniga
Orange, black, green and many other
colors

larghezza 80 cm
profondità 140 cm
altezza 63,5 cm
seduta 26 cm

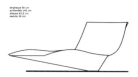

Lofty Poltrona

Armchair with steel structure and
base designed by P. Cazzaniga
Orange, black, green and many other
colors

larghezza 80 cm
profondità 75 cm
altezza 63 cm
seduta 29 cm

M1

Stackable chair designed by
P. Cazzaniga
Red, black, yellow and many other
colors

52x74x49

New Case

Modular storage furniture designed
by F. Bettoni and B. Fattorini
Aluminum and aluminum with white
fronts

Random

Bookshelf with two-inch-thick boards
designed by Neuland
White

Minotti

Via Independenza 152
PO Box 61, 20036 Meda (MI), Italy
P: +39 362 343 499
info@minotti.it
www.minotti.it

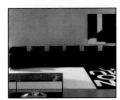

Carnaby Double

Chaise longue with metal structure
and upholstered in leather design by
Annette Hinterwirth
Black, brown and many other colors
or combinations

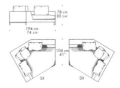

Hamilton Islands

Sofa modules upholstered in fabric or
leather designed by Rodolfo Dordoni
Beige, white, black and many other
colors

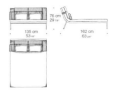

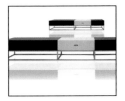

Harrison

Table with aluminum structure and
smoked-glass top designed by
Rodolfo Dordoni
Smoked glass

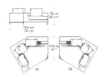

Richards
Armchair designed by Rodolfo
Dordoni
Black, beige and other colors

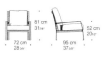

MK
Av. Las Condesas 11.400, oficina 34
Santiago de Chile, Chile
P: +56 678 9000
contacto@mk.cl
www.mk.cl

Mo by Martínez Otero
Av. de Pontevedra 97
36689, A Estrada, Pontevedra, Spain
Tel: +34 98 659 00 72
info@martinezotero.com
www.martinezotero.com

Copenhagen
Line of benches and containers
designed by Tobias Jacobsen
Green, dark green, red, dark brown
and white

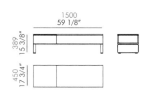

Horizon Systems
Modular storage system designed by
Pearson Lloyd
Green, gray, fuchsia, black, white
and other colors

Infinity
Table with two tops, designed by
Pearson Lloyd
Steel with wood or MDF in orange or
gray

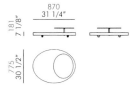

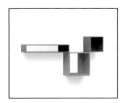

Mirror Mirror
Shelving system designed by
Pearson Lloyd
Plywood or MDF in different colors

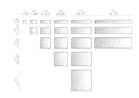

Screenwall
Separating screens designed by
Tobias Jacobsen
White and black

Mobles 114 Barcelona
Riera dels Frares 24
08907 L'Hospitalet de Llobregat, Barcelona, Spain
P: +34 93 260 01 14
mobles114@mobles114.com
www.mobles114.com

Flod
Stool designed by Azuamoliné
White, gray, orange and pistachio

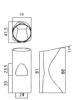

Modus Head Office
Unit 5, Westcombe Trading Estate, Station Road
Ilminster, Somerset TA19 9DW, United Kingdom
P: +44 460 57465
info@modusfurniture.co.uk
www.modusfurniture.co.uk

Os
Chair and armchair designed by
Jonathan Prestwich
Red, black and metal

Molteni & C
Rossini 50, 20034 Giussano (MI), Italy
P: +39 036 23 591
info@molteni.it
www.molteni.it

505
Storage system with multiple combinations designed by Luca Meda
Wood and lacquered in white, yellow and other colors

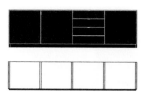

909
Chests of drawers in wood or lacquered designed by Luca Meda
Wood, ochre, white and other colors

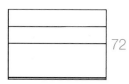

72

3030
Chests of drawers with sliding top that can transform into a writing desk designed by Hannes Wettstein
Natural or dyed gray oak, wengue and mutenye

Clip
Bed with structure upholstered in fabric or leather designed by Patricia Urquiola
Yellow, gray, black and many other colors

Convivio
Multi-combination storage solutions designed by Ferruccio Laviani
Black, green, white and other colors

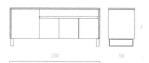

Diamond

Table with aluminum structure
designed by Patricia Urquiola
Aluminum, lacquered in white, black
or pearl, gray oak or wengue

Glove

Chairs and armchairs designed by
Patricia Urquiola
Orange, yellow, lilac, green and many
other colors

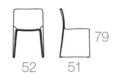

52   51   79

Lean

Chair with padded back, upholstered
in fabric or leather designed by
Rodolfo Dordoni
Mustard, black and many other
colors and finishes

Less

Table with metal structure designed
by Jean Nouvel
Lacquered in different colors or metal
with wood top

Skin

Sofa with innovative technology and
finishes in leather or felt designed by
Jean Nouvel
White, black and other colors

w. 247 – d. 96 – h. 67 cm
w. 97 1/4" – d. 37 3/4" – h. 26 3/8"

Move
www.move.it

Müller Möbel
Hummel-Müller OHG
Werner-von-Siemens Str. 6
86159 Augsburg, Germany
P: +49 8215 976 738
info@mueller-moebel.com

Classic Line BT 43
Metal bar furniture
Red, blue and many other colors

112 x 60 x 125
work surface 95

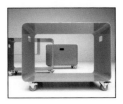

Mobile Line Trolley RW 107
Module with wheels and door
Green, red, pink, white and other
colors

60 x 40 x 46,5

Mobile Line Sideboard RW 400
Sideboard
Green, black, gray and other colors

90 x 40 x 97

Offecct
Box 100
SE-543 21 Tibro, Sweden
P: +46 504 415 00
support@offecct.se
www.offecct.se

King
Two-tone armchair designed by
Thomas Sandell
Multiple color combinations

46

Paco Capdell (Sillerías Alacuás)
Pol. Ind. La Garrofera s/n
PO BOX 32, 46970 Alacuás, Valencia, Spain
P: +34 96 150 20 50
info@pacocapdell.com
www.pacocapdell.com

Éboli
Chair with wooden back and
upholstered seat designed by
Vicente Soto
Black, white and other colors and
patterns

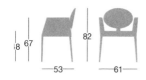

8 67   82

—53—   —61—

Hit
Chair with upholstered seat and back
designed by Vicente Soto
White, black, orange and other colors

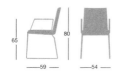

65   80

— 59 —   — 54 —

312C / 313C

Pedini
Via Aspio 8
61030 Lucrezia di Catoceto (PU), Italy
P: +39 721 899 988
info@pedini.it
www.pedini.it

Performa Möbel & Design GmbH
Marbacher Straße 54
74385 Pleidelsheim, Germany
P: +49 7144 898 869
welcome@performa.de
www.performa.de

Performanuf
Collection of tables with undulating
tops enabling them to slide
Gray, pink, white and other colors
and combinations

153

Perobell
Av. Arraona 23
08206 Sabadell, Barcelona, Spain
P: +34 93 745 79 00
info@perobell.com
www.perobell.com

Chicago
Modular bench system with
aluminum sheet structure designed
by Joan Gaspar
Red, black and other colors

Porro Industria Mobili Srl

Via per Cantù 35
22060 Montesolaro (CO), Italy
P: +39 317 80 237
info@porro.com
www.porro.com

Beam

Tempered glass and polished
aluminum tables designed by
Piero Lissoni
Oak. Also lacquered white in
rectangular version

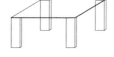

Ferro

Curved and welded metal ironing
board designed by Piero Lissoni

L. 180 cm H. 73 cm P. 85 cm

Nouvelle Vague

Chaise longue composed of chair
and pouf designed by Christophe
Pillet
Off-white, black and China red

Punt Mobles

Islas Baleares 48
46988 Fuente del Jarro, Valencia, Spain
P: +34 96 134 32 70
www.puntmobles.es
puntmobles@puntmobles.es

Camaleó

Modular shelving system
Wood or lacquered in black, green
and other colors

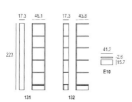

Literatura

Sliding shelves with wheels designed
by Vicent Martínez
Wood or lacquered in black, green
and other colors

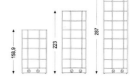

PenjArt

Coat stand designed by Vicent
Martínez
Aluminum and leather in various
colors

Rafemar

Pol. Ind. Bufalvent, Ap. Correos 98
Miquel Servet 40-42
08240 Manresa, Barcelona, Spain
P: +34 93 878 48 10
rafemar@rafemar.com
www.rafemar.com

Blocs

Modular shelving
Cherry wood, oak or ebony

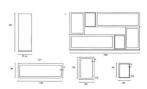

Charlie

Collection of coffee tables with
finishes in wood, matte lacquer and
shiny lacquer
Green, white and other colors

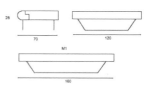

Prima

Collection of tables with stainless
steel metal leg
Cherry wood, walnut or oak

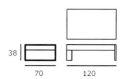

Roca

Av. Diagonal 513
08029 Barcelona, Spain
P: +34 93 366 12 00
infosan@roca.net
www.roca.es

Scavolini

Via Risara 60/70-74/78
61025 Montelabbate (Pu), Italy
P: +39 721 443 333
contact@scavolini.com
www.scavolini.com

Flux

Kitchen system designed by Giugiaro
Design
Brown, red, lilac and other colors

Schiffini Mobili Cucine SpA

Via Genova 206
19020 Ceparana (SP), Italy
P: +39 187 9501
info@schiffini.it
www.schiffini.it

G.Box

Kitchen system from the Emporium
collection, designed by Guiliano
Giaroli
Glass, marble, black and other colors
and finishes

Sphaus

Via A. Vespucci 4
20038 Seregno (MI), Italy
P: +39 362 330 355
sphaus@sphaus.com
www.sphaus.com

00.209

Rectangular table in two sizes with
MDF top designed by Filippo
Dell'Orto
Red, green, white, black and other
colors

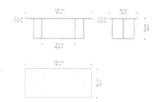

76er

Table with MDF top, designed by
Diego Sferrazza
Black, red, gray, white and other
colors

Cells

Coffee tables designed by Enrico
Buscemi and Piergiorgio Leone
Red, black, green, white and other
colors

Flirstones

Irregular chairs designed by Barbara
Golterman
Gray, black, beige and other colors

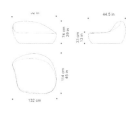

Fractal

Shelves with asymmetrical doors
designed by Claudio Loavadina
Blue, red, white, orange and other
colors

Lunar
Round dining table designed by
Manolo Bossi
White, black, red and other colors

T2
Coffee table designed by Luca Casini
Gray, green, orange and other colors

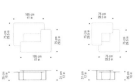

Stone Designs
Cordón 10
28005 Madrid, Spain
P: +91 540 03 36
info@stone-designs.com
www.stone-designs.com

Elephant
Fiberglass and lacquered polyester
stool
Orange, blue and other colors

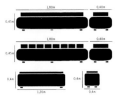

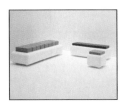

Multiugum
Lacquered bench with upholstered
polystyrene foam cushions
White with red, orange and other
colors

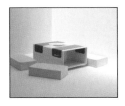

Self-service
Lacquered DM, upholstered
polyurethane foam cushions
White, orange and other colors

Stua

Polígono 26, E
20115 Astigarraga, San Sebastián, Spain
P: +34 94 355 60 02
stua@stua.com
www.stua.com

Onda

Ergonomic stool designed by Jesús
Gasca
White combined with black, orange
and other colors

Toscoquattro

Via Sila 40
59100 Prato, Italy
P: +39 574 815 535
toscoquattro@toscoquattro.it
www.toscoquattro.it

Viable

112 Cremer Business Centre
37 Cremer Street
London E2 8HD, United Kingdom
P: +44 207 729 4144
mail@viablelondon.com
www.viablelondon.com

Viccarbe Hábitat S.L.

Trav. Camí el Racó 1, Pol. Ind. Norte Beniparrell
46469 Valencia, Spain
P: +34 96 120 10 10
info@viccarbe.com
www.viccarbe.com

Aspa

Table with MDF top and steel
structure designed by Francesc Rifé
Lacquered base in black or white
and top in different finishes

Holy Day

Collection of tables designed by
Jean-Marie Massaud
White, black, red and other colors

Last Minute

Stools designed by Patricia Urquiola
White and black

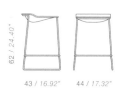

43 / 16.92"   44 / 17.32"

Mass

Modular sofa designed by Francesc
Rifé
White, gray and other colors

R1

Stackable chair with detachable
covers, designed by Francesc Rifé
Wood, yellow, black, white and other
colors

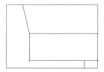

44 / 17.32"   52 / 20.47"

Visionnaire
IPE Cavalli
Via Mattei 1
40069 Zola Predosa (BO), Italy
P: +39 516 186 322
ipe@ipe.it
www.ipe.it

Vitra
info@vitra.com
www.vitra.com

Coconut Chair
Chair designed by George Nelson
White, orange, black and other colors

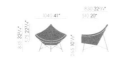

Metal Side Table
Tables designed by Ronan & Erwan
Bouroullec
Red, black and other colors

Self Shelf
Modular shelving unit designed by
Ronan & Erwan Bouroullec
White combined with various colors

Zana
Via Vicenza 7
20036 Meda (CO), Italy
P: +39 362 341 154
info@zanaitalia.it
www.zanaitalia.com

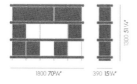

Dado
Bedside table in lacquered wood
Natural wood, black, green and other
colors

Zanotta
Via Vittorio Veneto 57
20054 Nova Milanese, Italy
P: +39 362 4981
zanottaspa@zanotta.it
www.zanotta.it

Dama

Armchair upholstered in leather or
fabric designed by Emaf Progetti
Brown, white and other colors

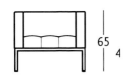

65
4

Desco

Outdoor table designed by Emaf
Progetti
White and black

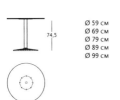

74,5

Ø 59 см
Ø 69 см
Ø 79 см
Ø 89 см
Ø 99 см

Evolution

Armchair with aluminum swivel base
designed by Ora Ïto
White and black

119

40

— 69 —   — 80 —

Gamma

Modular sofa with steel structure
designed by Emaf Progetti
Yellow, beige, white and other colors

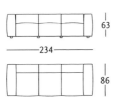

63

— 234 —

86

Giravolta

Extending table designed by Emaf
Progetti
Oak or oak dyed in wengue

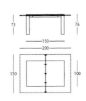

73   76

—150—
—200—

150   100

Hillroad
Armchair upholstered in fabric or
leather designed by Christophe Pillet
Orange, gray and many other colors

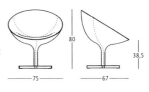

80
38,5
75
67

Level
Irregular bookshelf designed by
Arik Levy
Wood with gray, red and green

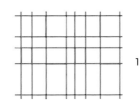

1

Time
Table with shiny lacquered finish
designed by Prospero Rasulo
Red, black, white and other colors

50

Yuki
Armchair designed by Christophe
Pillet
Black

81
71
82

Zeritalia
Division of Curvet Ambienti SpA
Via Della Resistenza sc
61030 Calcinelli di Saltara (PU), Italy
P: +39 721 878 511
zeritalia@zeritalia.com
www.zeritalia.com

Kurl
Modular shelving unit made in tinted
glass designed by Karim Rashid
Green, pink, blue and other colors

Architects and Designers

123dv Architectuur & Consult bv
St-Jobsweg 20 A
3024 EJ, Rotterdam, The Netherlands
P: +31 10 478 20 64
info@123dv.nl
www.123dv.nl
Loft Lloydkwartier
Photos: Christian de Bruijne

Anima LLC Architecture & Design
20 Jay Street, Suite 308
Brooklyn, NY 11201, USA
P: +1 718 643 0905
mail@anima.cc
www.anima.cc
Joralmon Street Loft
Photos: Anima LLC Architecture & Design

CJ Studio
Floor 6, N. 54 Lane 260 Kwang Fu South Road
Taipei, Taiwan
P: +2 2773 8366
cj@shi-chieh-lu.com
www.shi-chien-lu.com
Tsai Residence
Photos: Marc Gerritsen

**Double G Flora de Gastines & Anne
Geistdoerfer
Architecture, Interieur et Design**
50 rue de Sévigné
75003 Paris, France
P: +39 1 42 78 17 56
flora@doubleg.fr
www.doubleg.fr
Apartment in Paris
Photos: André Thoraval

Filippo Bombace
Via Monte Tomatico 1
00141 Rome, Italy
P: +39 686 898 266
info@filippobombace.com
www.filippobombace.com
Apartment in Rome
Pink House
Photos: Luigi Fileciti

**Fnp Architekten – Fischer Naumann
Partnerschaft**
Heilbronner Straße 39a
70191 Stuttgart, Germany
P: +49 7113 058 006
info@fischer-naumann.de
www.fischer-naumann.de
Haeckenhaus Hotel
Photos: Zooey Braun

Gerold Peham
Ignaz Härtl Strasse 9, 5020 Salzburg, Austria
P: 43 662 641 152
office@nomadhome.com
www.nomadhome.com
Nomad Home
Photos: Nomad Home Trading GmbH

Götz Keller
Loft in Berlin
Photos: Werner Huthmacher

I29 Office for Design
Industrieweg 29
1115 AD Duivendrecht, The Netherlands
P: +31 20 695 61 20
info@i29.nl
www.i29.nl
Heart of Home
Photos: I29 Office for Design

India Mahdavi
5 rue Las Cases
75007 Paris, France
P: +33 1 45 51 63 89
studio@indiamahdavi.com
www.india-mahdavi.com

Karim Rashid
357 West 17th St.
New York, NY 10011, USA
P: +1 212 929 8657
office@karimrashid.com
www.karimrashid.com

Lucia Borrego
Amado Nervo 12, 2° D
28007 Madrid, Spain
interiorismo@luciaborrego.com
www.luciaborrego.com
Loft in Madrid
Photos: Jordi Canosa

Matali Crasset Productions
26 rue de Buisson Saint Louis
75010 Paris, France
P: +33 1 42 40 99 89
matali.crasset@wanadoo.fr
www.matalicrasset.com

Michael P. Johnson Design Studio
7160 East Sierra Vista Road
Cave Creek, USA
P: +1 480 488 2691
michael@mpjstudio.com
www.mpjstudio.com
Silverman Residence
Photos: Bill Timmerman

Nico Heysse
De Neckstraat 22
1081 Brussel, Belgium
P: +32 476 31 09 68
nicoheysse@skynet.be
XL Loft
Photos: Laurent Brandajs

Orefelt Associates
43 Pall Mall Deposit, 124-128 Barlby Road
London W10 6BL, United Kingdom
P: +44 208 96 02560
mail@orefelt.demon.co.uk
Apartment in London
Photos: Alberto Ferrero

Ptang Studio Ltd
Rm 603-604 Harry Industrial Building
49-51 Au Pui Wan Street, Sha Tin
New Territories, Hong Kong
P: +852 2669 1577
office@ptangstudio.com
www.ptangstudio.com
Silverman Residence
Photos: Bill Timmerman

Ronan & Erwan Bouroullec Design
23 rue du Buisson Saint-Louis
75010 Paris, France
P: +33 142 00 52 11 (fax)
info@bouroullec.com
www.bouroullec.com

Stephen Varady Architecture
PO Box 105 (14 Lackey Street)
St. Peters NSW 2044, Sydney, Australia
P: +61 2 9516 4044
sva@stephenvarady.com
www.stephenvarady.com
Mitchinson Residence
Larson Kelly Residence
Photos: Stephen Varady

Teresa Sapey
Francisco Campos 13
28002 Madrid, Spain
P: +34 91 745 08 76
estudio4@teresasapey.com
www.teresasapey.com
Isoleé
Photos: Jordi Miralles

The Apartment Creative Agency
101 Crosby Street
New York, NY 10012, USA
P: +1 212 219 3661
info@theapt.com
www.theapt.com
The Y Apartment
Photos: Michael Weber

Unamanu
Val San Martino Superiore 49
10131 Torino, Italy
P: +39 118 399 789
info@unamanu.it
www.unamanu.it
Il Salasso
Photos: Andrea Martiradonna

747